The Semicolon

Jan Rothschein

Published by Jan Rothschein, 2022.

While every precaution has been taken in the preparation of this book, the publisher assumes no responsibility for errors or omissions, or for damages resulting from the use of the information contained herein.

THE SEMICOLON

First edition. November 27, 2022.

Written by Jan Rothschein.

Table of Contents

INTRODUCTION

If you're reading this it's actually not that late, I'm glad to let you know I got better,however these poems were written by me when I was very dark state of mind as you can tell from their subject matter. Originally most of those poems were intended to be used as a goodbye letter or released after I'm gone, hence the name "semicolon[1]". Luckily that didn't happen , with that said I sincerely hope that the poems are not that relatable for you, and I hope you read those without thinking negatively I also hope that my poems will try to brighten and change your view on the world and mental well-being of you and others.

this book is divided into a few small parts, each starts with a minimalistic illustration done by me, which is trying to hint at the subject matter of the part. Not every chapter has the same amount of poems sadly so I hope it doesn't bother anyone and I hope my decision to divide the book was fruitful for the readers understanding of different subject matters in the semicolon.

They say depressed people are good at art and that's the quote I'll use to wrap this messy intro to an even messier book. Sincerely

"What occupies the toughts of a man if not his flaws?"
IS THAT ME? THAT CAN NOT BE ME, I GOTTA WORK HARDER

GREEN TEA AND GUM

Green tea and gum became a tradition
to my life they were a harmful addition
then came avoiding condiments
in desperate need for compliments
what did I think going through all this?
sometimes wished that I didn't exist
ignored when It got hard to go and piss
or when the colour faded from my lips
saw all the signs but I didn't care
Slowly lost tiny bits of my hair
as I sit desperately on the chair
trying to avoid my mum's judging stare
trying to avoid all confused gazes
everytime i went through my food crazes
avoided eating food
that I normally would
wasn't up to no good
always in a bad mood
due to being rude
I lost everyone's help.
Craving junk food
played with my mental health
even tough I've felt my skin breathe,
in all of my clothes
I still did believe
extra calories to be kilos.
If I knew then what I know now
knew how my metabolism would down
how my image would get messed up,
leaving to me being stressed up

most of my days
I'm still met with a confused gaze
cause i start acting weird
when my body doesn't get enough praise
some days I wanna hide
not even step into the sun
it's the days I'm feeling wide
feeling like I weight a ton
wish I never lied,
when people ask what's wrong
and wish I never tried
the magic of green tea and gum...

REALLY ME

Looking in the mirror
confused at what I see
trying to get my sight clearer
but I know I'm not seeing me.
I can get around
and call myself big all day long
next day I'm crying loud,
just because I don't feel that strong.
And my friends said I've got issues
all that healthy eating missused
nights spent watering up tissues
and I still can't find a way out
compliments fly clear and loud
but I chose to react with doubt.
I'm trapped in a jaw that just ain't devouring,
it gets worse with every drink that I'm pouring.
people talk to me
and say my goals are hard to figure.
but my goal is only
to kill the person in the mirror...

MY LOVELY COMPANION

I used to have this wonderful friend
    I believe she was called Ana
    Ana was convinced life would end
    if you ate a Banana
    Ana would plague your mind with hate
    Ana would make you stay up late
    Ana would refuse a drop of rum
    just to down two packs of gum
    Ana tought that she did right
    by suppressing her appetite
    Ana would never call your body good
    she would always stress about food
    She would always put her diet first
    She would say hunger's just disguised thirst
    Ana would put your friends in shock
    she would keep all your urges at lock
    She knew the portions of every meal
    She may have preached health, but did she heal
    see Ana's body although it's "pretty"
    she often did feel very shitty
    losing pounds week by week
    got her body pretty weak
    all her bones were crumbling
    and her innards were rumbling
    as she humbly declines another meal
    she asks god "when will I heal?"
    all gum and green tea got her body shaking
    she can't keep stillness
    the news to her will be heartbreaking
    once she realises it's an illness

will she ever fight that feeling?
will she refuse all forms of healing?
I'm afraid it is too late
ana's body's melting down.
while her surroundings chose to wait,
and compliment her, ignoring her frown.
Ana spent her last days tied to a chair.
in the end she lost her hair
and the world slowly got rid of her.
Though there's one thing I should make clearer
she's waiting behind every mirror
hiding behind every dresser
looking for a new weak vessel
a teenager who feels like they don't fit their dress
is an easy target for Ana to posses
a teenager who struggles with self
can quickly become Ana herself...

Tell me why did I become strong?
why did I listen to every hype song?
why did I work out for so long?
and still my image feels wrong
tell me why did I do thousands of burpees
cried over a pack of smarties
then did another thousand of burpees.
Why have I skipped every party
and still I do hate my body
tell me why do I strive to win
over the voice from within
why do I strive to be thin?
just to hate every inch of my skin
tell me why did I even try
avoided getting drunk or high
all the days where I lied
lied about how much I ate
when it's myself that I hate
why did I endure this pain?
why do I harm my own brain?
seeing the mirror makes me wanna die
Car reflections make me wanna cry.
Why did I believe I had to run
everyday after eating something fun?
why did I always go walking?

just to avoid people talking
talking about my weight loss magic
when we both know it's tragic
cause when I get told
my body's not worthy of galleries
I mentally fold
thinking of how to burn more calories
I sit alone in my room of empty dishes
empty promises, unfulfilled wishes.
I'm sitting here pondering if it was worth it
so much anguish just to never feel „perfect"...

"Where do souls of
suicidal angels go?"

"Where do souls of
suicidal angels go?"

HEAVEN

Cars are like chariots
to heaven or hell
intention or inexperience
who will even tell
if the one who has had enough
jumps into the road
once he does the final bluff
he'll just spread like a toad
no one will go and help the driver still
help him get rid of survivors guilt since he was going hundred ten
He couldn't stop to save a man
two young souls
not one was over twenty seven
yet now I suppose
not one will get to heaven
heaven allows those who dare
yet heaven allows only those who care.
Heaven waters all withered flowers
so why didn't they give that man power?
why did they let him suffer through life?
why did they trouble his beautiful wife?
why didn't god send him bliss through the air?
how do we even know a god is there?
and if he's there, how do we know he cares
how do we know he doesn't just stare
doesn't just laugh at our puny affairs.
He sees our pain choses not to improve it
no one saw him and no one can prove it
he saw sysyphus's rock and refused to move it
if god is really there how can he prove it?

• • • •

If god is there I would like to meet him
if he is real I would like to greet him
pour us two cups full of heavenly wine
show him every church, cathedral shrine
show him that our love for him is deep
but also make him hear humanity's weeps
if god is real I'd love to see him myself
sit him down nicely while I ask for help
ask for help nicely I don't wanna fall
ask him to bring us what could save us all...

THOUGHTS IN THE DARK

Riding through the city
    and I feel a bit shitty
    because everyone I see
    always looks better
    why do I gotta be me
    trying to send god a letter
    or just reach him via e mail
    make him make my life not derail
    trynna hit on heaven's line
    attempt to stop my decline
    even tough i might appear fine
    I am mentally offline
    wondering about what to hate about myself today?
    my body?my face? or how much I weigh?
    living like this feels like a crime
    and it's filling me with rage
    but believe me there was a time
    where I tried to make a change
    and believe me there were times
    I even did things that you'd consider strange
    I've came very far but my mind's on fire
    why ain't I a star or why ain't I desired.
    Went through many phases
    some better some worse
    wanna blow myself to pieces
    to try end the curse
    but when I'm too far gone who will miss me
    who'll even notice that I found the end that fits me.
    Tired of people acting like friends cause your good for them
    stop pretending to care see the stars, then shoot for them

sick of being viewed like a low hanging fruit for them
but I just can't be arsed to just go up and be rude to them.
Not trying to let it show but I'm tired of pretending
pretending to smile while on the verge of ending
the verge of ending it all
in a dark abyss I fall
fall down in its depths forever.

· · · ·

Call these rhymes whatever
    but you cant call them pretty
    came home from the city
    and I still feel a bit shitty...

Sorry if i come off as a bother
    but nowadays its Hard
    screw this life
    I want another.

        Sorry if i come off as a burden
        but all the negativity inside
        has me burning
        made some mistakes but im learning
        open up my eyes see the tide
        and its turning.

Sorry if i differ from the old me
but i just want you to hold me
without you im dying slowly
this life used to be so holy
but now all my so called homies
are acting like they dont know me
that has me feeling lonely.

        Sorry if i come off as presistent
        suicidal toughts
        I dont know if i can resist them
        cause i just want you close
        want your blood flowing in my system
        but you dont seem to listen.

Sorry if i come off as if i need help
but i really need to control my health
I figured out the way i treat myself
might be the reason i wanna delete myself.

        Sorry if i come off as boring
        but im tired of the constant ignorng
        i dont feel like having fun

Going to load the gun
and then start snoring...

Hey man how are you?
    been a long time since we last met
    no please don't do
    don't ask me the question I dread
    I beg you don't do that
    don't try to look into my head
    cause all you'll find is noises
    loud whistles and deep voices
    effects of over and underproduction
    and thoughts of self destruction.
    Don't try to play deep
    don't act like you care
    you were never there
    when I was losing sleep
    you tried to treat me as a joke
    when I told you my secrets
    once you finally watch me choke
    on that tree is when you'll regret
    regret spreading all the lies
    regret our friendship being a disguise
    regret attacking me by surprise
    regret being the reason someone cries
    now that you're the reason someone died.
    Will you rue the way you made him
    the same way he rues his end
    will you rue how you used to hate him
    but yet you played pretend
    made him feel like he's worth
    but now he's in the dirt
    yeah that man's forever gone

took his own life
shook his family to the bone
had no time for a wife
gone with no house to own
he wasn't even 22
now you're standing alone
regretting what you made him do
you wished for it as a joke but he made it true
so now there is just a question for you
will you rue?

III
"Altough we wish all we can none of us can return what once was?"

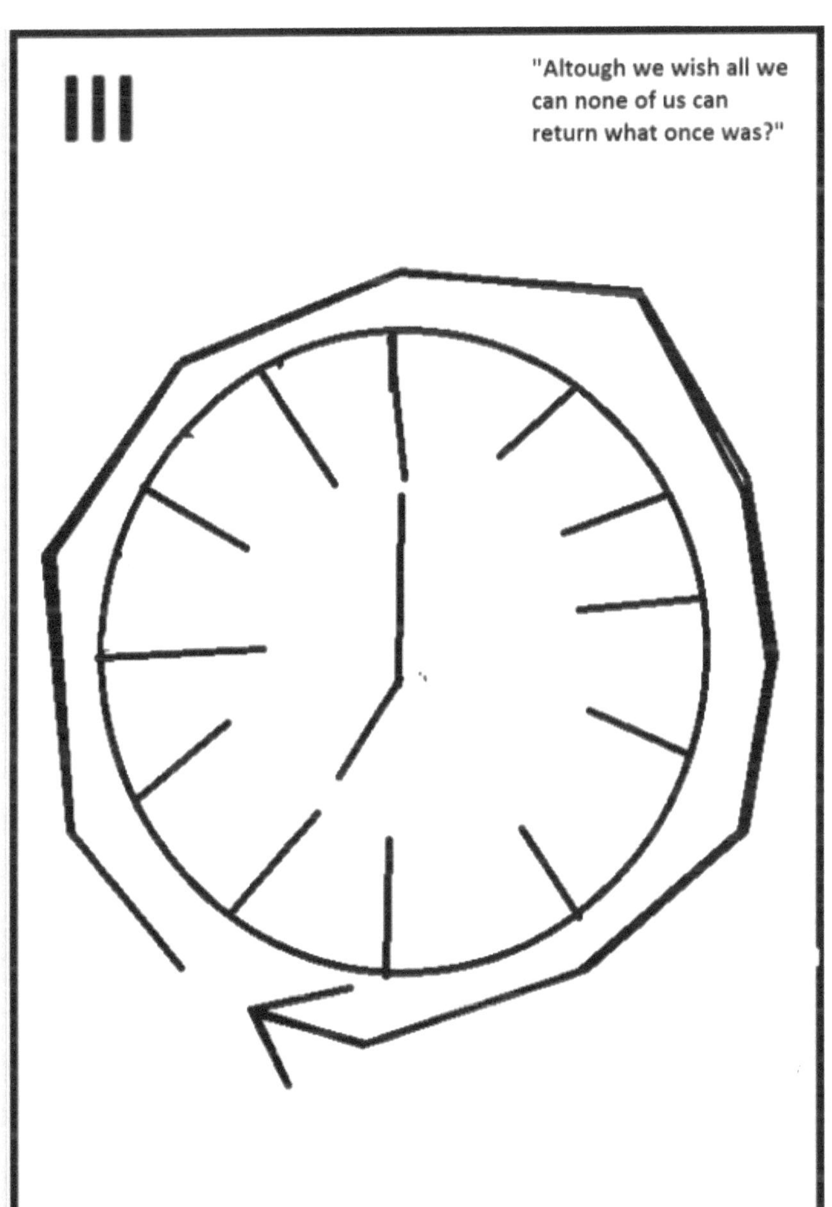

17

NOTHING IS FOREVER

You lost some weight
    it came back with a smile
    you fell for some bait
    now you'll feel bad for a while
    you've made a friend
    well they don't like you that much
    as in the end
    they'll just see you as a crutch
    they'll tell you you're great
    that there's nothing you lack
    then you hear them hate
    wanting a noose around your neck
    it might be to late
    to realize that they never liked you back
    they just talked behind your back
    but they don't all hate you
    might just be a few
    and no one wants to date you
    you're no one's center of view.
    Remember the times
    you always rocked a smile
    and felt like you're in your prime
    gotta say it's been a while
    where did that smile go
    did it become forgotten
    it was before you saw your belly grow
    and your teeth get rotten
    your face got deformed too
    you're struggling but nobody asked
    every morning you

contemplate wearing a mask
wearing a mask for the rest of your life
might be better than hurting yourself with a knife.
Plus now you can't leave the house because
you want a magic mouse to bring back what once was
but there's no such thing as magic
messing with "spells" always ends tragic.

. . . .

There's no one to blame but yourself
	your bad decisions put you through more hell
	but no one will come as your saviour
	it's only you that can do this favour
	said favour is saving yourself from going crazy
	I beg you on my knees please don't be lazy
	save yourself swim up from this sea of hate
	save yourself please before it's too late...

Could read at 7 and wondered why
    everyone saw me as a super guy
    What do I do with that skill now?
    all I was back then was a cash cow
    a display of my parent's ways
    a soul to never fade to gray
    twelve year later you check my room
    to witness me just awaiting doom
    would I have thought when I was little
    that I'd see school as a mental hospital
    institutes filled with empty souls
    empty streets, empty people, empty net empty goal.
    At 7 I could read and the world was bright
    I wonder who went and turned off the light?
    I wonder when I became scared to fight?
    I wonder when others made me flee on sight?
    Wonder when I stopped wanting to sleep at night?

      • • • •

At 7 years old my dad showed me "highway to hell"
                12 years later I am scared of myself.
    Who would've thought that I'd be scared of being bigger?
    Who would've thought I'd hate looking in the mirror?
    At 7 years old used to be scared of dogs.
              Now I'm scared of models in catalogues.
    At 7 years old me and my friends tried spells.
            12 years later I'd walk through seven hells
              just to try and become someone else...

NOSTALGIC MELANCHOLY

looking at an old picture
wondering where it went wrong
when did I get in the mixture
of feeling only weak or strong
how come now I get so tired
that I can barely read a book
my mental state is wired
to how i currently look
how come in the old times
it used to be so good
when the summer reeked of lime
and I wasn't scared of food.
Miss the time when I was younger
when I wasn't scared of hunger
although my frame looked a bit wider
at least I wasn't such an outsider
I miss the times so much it does hurt
back when I atleast knew my worth
when I still knew how people work.
Nowadays a good feeling is more rare
than a junkie on crack
for this I might get a weird stare
but I wish to go back.
I Wish to go back by atleast 4 years
doing that would dry all my present self's tears
doing that would clear all my present self's fears
i believe what would help my present self heal
is to go back to a time which didn't feel real...

It's Sunday,
how was your week?

On Monday,
you just felt very weak.

Came Tuesday,
you could barely even speak
to your friends in school
kinda made them seek
you to ask if you still see them as cool.

Then came Wednesday,
and you didn't get much sleep
but you didn't really think
much cause it wasn't that deep
you just had an energy drink.

then came Thursday,
time to work on your health
cause things are not fine
you looked at yourself
and started crying
you aren't satisfied
with what your labour brings
but it's the average life
so why stress over these things.

So on Friday,
you go out because you're bored
meet strangers and try to open their doors
but you can't stay sober
and you wish your life was over
but you keep it all in secret
keep doing things that you will regret.

and on Saturday,
you just spent the day sad
thinking of what you could've had
and kinda wishing you were dead
you got nothing done.
so that brings us back to question one
c'mon man I just wanna hear you speak
i just wanna know what did you do all week?

IV

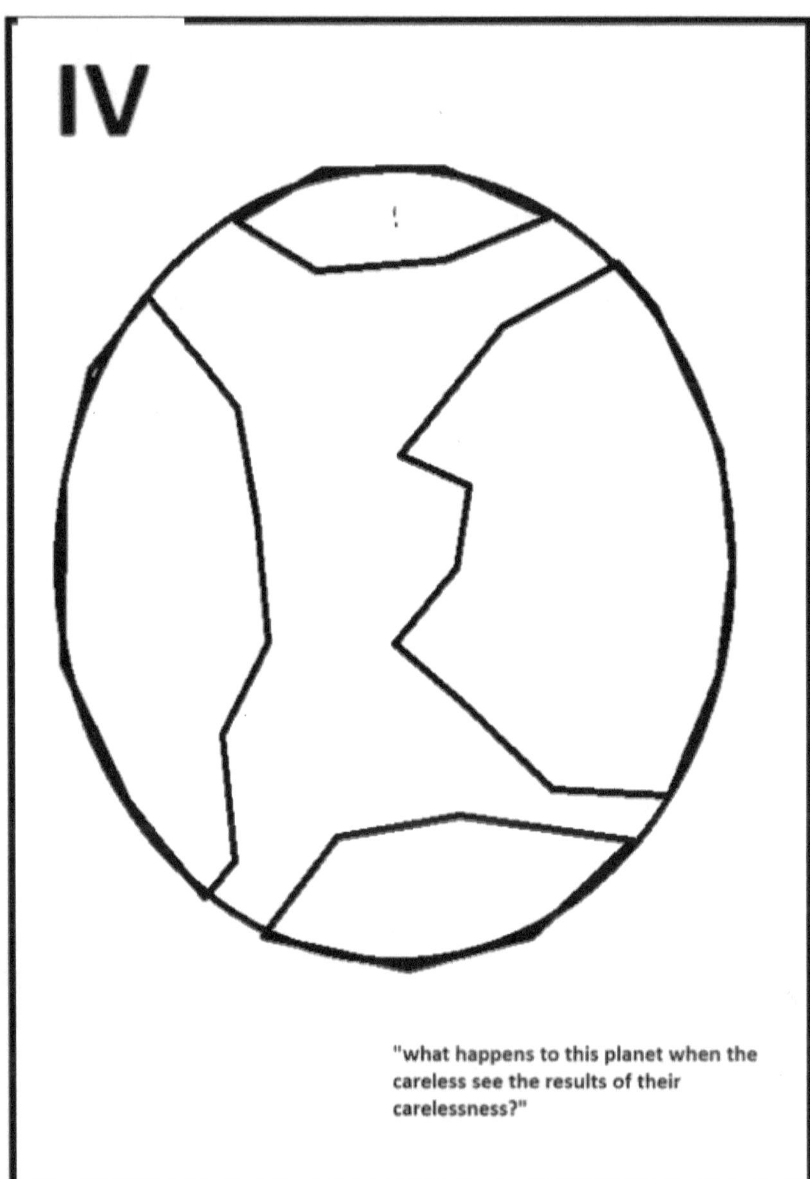

"what happens to this planet when the careless see the results of their carelessness?"

What makes a great actor?
It is not the ability to play
what makes a great actor
isnt always acting okay
what makes a great actor
isn't always having a busy day
what makes a great actor
is not always getting paid
what makes a great actor
is not pretending not to cry
what makes a great actor
is not refusing to wonder why
what makes a great actor
Is not avoiding to see the sky
well then what makes a great actor?
Well nobody knows
we think we all see great actors
watching movies and shows
but people nowadays rarely can see
what makes a great actor is not the tv
what makes actors great
is not the crowd
it's the ability to hate
to scream, to shout
to just run out
to vent, to yell
to go through pain,to go through hell
these are the things real actors do
the real actors are people
just like me and you...

In a world full of lies
and strange body doubles
just like drunk flies
collided our troubles
you tell me what's wrong
and I'll try to help
then I found out all along
I was taking to myself
nobody is there
to ever hear me crying
bet nobody would care
if they saw me dying
hiding the pain like shrimp
in a pan while it's frying
walking as if with a limp
getting weaker but I'm trying
scared of being called a wimp
so any help I am denying
scared of being called a bitch
but yet I'm here to the voice my wish.

I wish you could enter my head
the way I enter yours
if only you could forget what I said
if only we could shut the doors
you have me almost paralyzed
crawling on all fours
I regret that I analysed
every tought of yours
wish you could come and see
this odd twisted fantasy

in this messed up brain of me
I see our world as a sea
where dark blind souls
just crash into each other
just flying with no goals
no such thing as a mother
we spin like this non stop
round and round the planet
aiming to reach the top
and see the man who planned it...

Recently I realised
    I'm just a bag of meat
    in my bed as if I'm paralysed
    just looking at my feet
    i can see my flaws
    point them out one by one
    sometimes I just need a pause
    just to stare at the sun
    man we only live once
    why not pour a drink
    one day there might be more suns
    and one could even be pink
    that's the beauty of life
    we never know what's next
    and we never know where we're led.
    I still remember the night
    and all of the texts
    from the day we met
    the tears I've shed
    and the hair
    that fell out of my head
    the despair
    and the constant dread.
    But why care?
    About a person in a sea with others
    sea with a few billion sisters and brothers
    seven billion bags of meat
    who all have different passions
    it's pretty difficult to meet
    someone of exact same fashion

exact same taste in books, movies or music
everyone finds something else amusing.
Some like to play with words,
others like to look at birds,
some like to go on walks,
and some really hate small talk
some like to go on dates,
others enjoy going to sleep late,
some don't like looking in the mirror,
some would love their vision being clearer,
some like to excercise,
others enjoy extra fries.
That's why you should try sitting down and listening
to how we are wonderfully alike and so viciously distinct
seven billion ropes connected simply just by existing
made a tangled up yarn ball also known as earth...

SNOWING IN MARCH

It's the middle of march and it's snowing.
thinking about how many plants are growing.
even though outside every light is glowing.
at home I see a sight that's so harrowing.
So much mess on the bed
so much stress in my head
slowly learning to live
taking more than I give.
but where has that led me?
Many so called friends left me
although sometimes I'm glad
cause these things help you grow
but it can get quite sad
because no one's there when you're low
Trying to see life through a happy man's eyes
but everywhere I look there's something to despise
with every breath
comes a new death
with every rise
comes a quick fall
this slowly leads to the demise
of this planet and of us all.
Why is it snowing in the middle of march?
Why are negative emotions still at large?
When our leaders die, who do we put in charge?
Will Noah had to build another arch?
so many questions but not enough answers
it's snowing in march but atleast the sky looks handsome...

V
"Ask anyone if they are truly happy with being who they are, not many answers would be positive"
WHY CAN I NOT BE SOMEONE ELSE?
WHY AM I LIKE THIS?

Not good enough to hug
    not good enough to fuck
    not good enough to love,
                        good enough to not be treated rough
                            good enough to be called tough,
    not good enough to be admired
    not good enough to feel inspired
    not good enough to get asked to dance
    not good enough to have some confidence,
                                good enough to buy you a drink,
    not good enough to know what you think,
                            good enough not to feel my bones
                                good enough not to feel alone
                            good enough to feel safe at home,
    not good enough for texts on my phone,
                                good enough to go on walks,
    not good enough not to feel stalked,
                                good enough to take a shower,
    not good enough to feel power,
                                good enough to feel stylish
                                good enough to feel childish,
    not good enough to feel peace,
                            good enough to not be full of grease
                                good enough to have a head,
    not good enough to not be bad.

Bad enough to get bruised
bad enough to feel used
bad enough to be excused
bad enough to feel dizzy and confused
bad enough to feel like shit
bad enough to want to commit
bad enough not to be desired
bad enough to have my lunch expire
bad enough to always feel cold
bad enough to lack a hand to hold
bad enough to always feel lazy,

         not bad enough to go crazy,

bad enough to feel like falling,

      not bad enough to hear death calling
        not bad enough to stink
        not bad enough to drink,

bad enough to never feel pretty
bad enough for all things to end shitty,

        not bad enough to be broke,

bad enough to be taken as joke
bad enough to be eating too much
bad enough to be seen as just a crutch
bad enough to want to die
bad enough to want to cry
bad enough to always seek comfort in people
bad enough to see life a steep hill,

       not bad enough to require a sleep pill,

bad enough to crave that deep feel
that deep feeling of liberty
once I reach infinity...

I Envy the moon
    cause you think it's pretty
    I Envy the saloon
    it makes you like this city
    I Envy the sky
    it's the thing you always mention
    I Envy the fly
    she's your center of attention
    I Envy the bird
    cause it can move freely
    I Envy every word
    cause they can save lives, really
    I Envy the gods
    cause someone believes in them always
    I Envy the rods
    which are held by old people on cold days
    I wish to be the staff
    feel the old man's lack of worry
    he has lived a life of love
    it's the ending of his story
    I wish to be the thing
    that accompanies him to heaven.
    I wish that I could sing
    but my surroundings are deafened
    I envy the skinny, I envy the fat
    I envy the curvy, I envy the flat
    It might seem silly to say all that
    but they can look at themselves without feeling sad.
    I Envy the ground
    cause your feet always touch it
    I Envy the sound
    of the vacuum when you clutch it
    I Envy all that makes you happy
    what sane person wouldn't
    even thought it makes me feel crappy
    it does the thing i couldn't
    i envy a sleep pill
    cause people know it works
    I Envy the steeple
    it might be so cliche it hurts

but it's full of people
and all of them I see
are in some aspect a bit better than me
I Envy the people
who are what I'll never be.
I might have said to much
yet I don't envy the soil to one day hug me
cause who would wanna touch
a soul this dark and ugly...

I RELATE

I relate to the cars
I too am used to get people places
I relate to the stars
I too dissapear among many faces
I relate to your old dress
the way you used me to hide
your troubles and stress
replaced both with pride
then you pushed me aside.
I relate to the sun
the way I know when to come around
and the way I see you come down
try make a smile out your frown
yet when you see me close you run
I relate to the TV
the way you know I'm bad for you
yet you still wanna see me
and that honestly is dreamy.
I relate a book
the way you hesitate to give me a look
and the way I wanna leave you shook
i relate to food
saying that always annoyed me
but we both know what's good
yet you still choose to avoid me
I relate to your job
the way you kinda bore me
and don't take me serious
I'm treated like a drunken slob
the way you ignore me
yeah that makes me quite furious.
That's the list of the things
I wish I was once told
cause sometimes life just stings
those with hearts of gold
all the sufferings
that gods make us hold
even the strongest being
with time is meant to fold
all that mental beating

turns a gold heart cold...

37

I KILLED SOMEONE

I killed someone not with a knife
    I killed someone ended their life
    no trace of them to be found
    blood everywhere but no sound
    I killed them in a quiet place
    I watched the spirit leave their face
    I killed somebody in cold blood
    I killed them with a loud thud
    guilt in my head raising my hair
    I killed someone they looked very bad
    yet they didn't care
    they smiled and told me to "go ahead"
    I killed someone, took their head
    watched as they slowly cried and plead
    watched as they slowly screamed and bled
    watched them utter their last breath
    I killed someone they asked me to
    split their mind and soul in two
    I killed a man that was happy
    unconditionally happy.

• • • •

Maybe I was jealous of that
    how can he smile oh so often
    how can he not stress with life
    how come he has a lovely wife
    how come he has clear skin
    how come he looks scared to sin
    how come is his life a win

moments full of serotonin
people talk he doesn't listen
he's like the human medicine
I had a knife he didn't run
just kept staring at the sun
why he didnt he use his phone
just smiled cheekbone to cheekbone
i did what he asked me to
split a happy man in two
i did what you asked me to
killed a happy man for you .
I killed someone you all were there
I killed someone and didn't care
Killed someone, now his skin i wear
I killed the man that I once were...

A SCHOONER CALLED INSANITY

I let my emotions swing
    doing horrible things
    believing too many lies
    led me to cutting many ties
    don't get me wrong I love my friends
    i Always hate when our moment ends
    however no one deserves
    seeing me at my worst
    an emotional wreck
    lacking self respect
    Sometimes I talk to myself
    trying to find someone else to blame
    tell myself I don't need help
    convince myself it's a game
    yet at said game I do bad
    and that makes me pretty sad
    want to be out but I'm still in my room
    trying to punch a wall
    or trying to bend a broom
    just because of something small
    why do I explode over nothing
    all it takes is someone puffing
    or just chewing my food loud
    that makes me wanna shout.

        · · · ·

Something needs to change
    lately I've been acting strange
    that even the blind would see

that I lost control of me
lost control over what I feel
lost control over knowing what is real
so many emotions all changing at wheel
every situation they argue about who will wield it
fills my friends with frustration cause it makes me hard to deal with
Sadly I can't change,no way to clear my head
sadly it makes people wish we never met
i feel like there's no way to fix
my messy emotional mix
I can only begin dreaming
of the day when I stop screaming
dreaming of that final day
when all my thoughts fade to gray...

VI
WEIRD!
FAT!
Have you ever tried asking a tormented person to stand up? it is to no use, they mostly have reasons not to"
UGLY!
LATE !

[]

Why are you
	nice to me one day
	then mean to me the next
	how can't you
	see the things you say
	tend to make me stressed
	I took your insult with pride
	yet then at home I cried
	looking for what I did wrong
	to make your hatred for me that strong
	the thing I never see
	is the fault in you or me
	how'd your cold heart come to be
	was it your parents or the TV.
	You're like the king of this place
	everyone is meant to love you
	I wanna see the look on your face
	when someone gets above you
	when someone comes to take down
	your glued-on uncomfy crown
	do you even care
	that I go home with a frown.
	Got tadpoles in my hair
	from that time you tried to drown
	tried to drown me with your friends
	there was no mean of defense
	I just hoped that it would end
	wish i didn't have to pretend
	pretend that I like you too
	cause I know what you would do

if I told someone the whole truth.
Every night I prayed to die
instead of going to school
every night I asked myself "why?"
I do this just to feel "cool"
do this just to feel "in"
if I had three wishes from a jhinn
I'd instantly waste one away
i would wish to go
go back to that day
when winter still had snow
and we were about to make our paws meet
so just future me can say
"no i know the pain you'll cause me"..

DEAR MR.TEMPER

Your ways of showing anger
    make me feel like I'm danger
    every time I hear your screams
    I feel like I'm losing my dreams
    why do you have to be mean
    over the littlest thing
    if someone doesn't intervene
    we will watch our ship sink
    why don't you see I'm scared
    questioning if you ever cared
    when you call me a rude word
    just because I haven't heard
    heard what you said
    because you were in your bed
    talking quietly like a fox
    now I'll hide in a box
    your temper forces me to admit
    that you're always right
    cause I don't want to get hit
    don't want to get into a fight
    don't want to withstand another
    screaming session
    why do I even bother
    with your aggression
    there's gonna be a moment
    where I can't put up anymore
    and the possibility that it's crawling
    has me shaken to my core
    why can't you understand
    every word you angrily say
    just make me wanna stand
    very far away
    far away from you
    even though you mean a lot
    i hate when you do
    act like you're someone you're not
    and this is very tough
    because I don't know your past
    don't know if it was rough
    but if you don't change we won't last

don't know if your resentment
came from bad parenthood
but each time your belittlement
makes me question my manhood
makes me question if I'm good
enough to keep you calm
makes me blame myself
I should always warn
warn myself of the eruptions you cause
warn myself everytime you're in your anger's jaws...

WHY

Why?

Do you shower me with praise?
    Can't you see that I can't feel my face?

Why?

    Do you send me all those doves?
    Can't you see I'm struggling to feel loved?

Why?

    Did you wanna hold my hand?
    Don't you know I'm thinking of my end?

Why?

Did you want to touch my hair?
Then be the one to kick my chair
leave me hanging without air
just looking at me without a care
it's what I would've wanted,right ?
get out of a world this tight
reach the tunnel, feel so bright
bask forever in heaven's light
they say out of sight out of mind
then I think you must be blind
because while I thought you're my partner in crime
you didn't bother giving me a digit of your time
your actions hurt, they sting like blades
and all your words hit like a truck
thought you were my lucky ace
turns out I'm just out of luck
now that you finally wonder
why do we both think about leaving
it soon hits like thunder
our punishment is breathing

47

breathing living on this planet
knowing our life's not like we planned it
spinning round like god's twisted dancers
with so many questions but no answers...

I'm tired
    every week I change my pace
    cause i hate
    being used as a feel good button
    tired of being the place
    an issue can be put on
    but I guess it's fate
    that I live to make the poor feel rich
    I guess it's late
    to realize my whole life I was a bridge
    for people to cross
    sadly I was just a one way route
    a bridge that says "I feel bad for you".
    Some nights
    I'm tired
    tired of being used as a wall
    tired of people ignoring my calls
    tired of shedding a light on my issues
    just to see them clearer
    it isn't that I miss you
    I just hate myself in a mirror
    sometimes I am breaking down in lectures
    most times I avoid taking pictures.
    Pictures of myself
    are only old ones on my shelf
    from when nothing could go wrong
    wondering where has this time gone
    but that's stuff nobody knows
    cause their interest never shows
    they're here just to hear my advice

then they dissapear like flies
flies in winter
wondering when will I feel like a winner
when will I feel like I deserved to eat diner.
I'm tired
tired of seeing what have I become
sometimes I wanna end everything what I've begun
yet I'm tired of seeing myself this defeated
but I put all the blame
on the way I was treated
when my inner flame
still was burning bright and clear
when I wasn't called insane
and when I lived with no fear
this definitely isn't the way God planned it
but I'm tired of being a person on this planet...

A TRIP THROUGH MY HEAD

There is a tall white palace
    inside of my mind
    I saved you a chalice
    so come and step inside
    come straight, make your way
    through this colorful disarray
    let's shroud ourselves in illusion
    to avoid all confusion

    .

    There's a small black palace
    inside of my head
    mostly surrounded by malice
    and covered in dread
    entering that place is what I deem a test
    this palace never hosted a single proper guest
    everyone who saw
    the inside of the place
    is said to grab a claw
    and get rid of their face
    tis' a place of madness
    in the back of my head
    its fences reek of sadness
    and all its hosts are dead.
    It takes a little power
    and despair is no more
    once you see a tower
    shining near a shore
    in the corner of my mind
    a shining lighthouse stands there
    on top of which you may find

glimpses of days bright and fair.
At the end of your journey
there should be a gate
there's a guard concerned he
concerned he about your fate
if you chose to access
through the gate don't wear a dress
at the other end there's just swamp and sludge
my mind is a mess
yet who are guests to judge...

VII
"Where do we draw the line between a bad habit and self destruction?"
18+
NOT
ENO
UG

Here I am spending my late nights
    doing mindless lefts and rights
    sold my life to dating sites
    is she bad or is she nice?
    this one has lots of coat hangers
    this one has pretty high standards
    this one looks like her spirit's weak
    this one's way out of my league
    this one says she lives pretty near
    this one has bruises on her ear
    so many choices and I get none
    every rejection is like shot of a gun
    i used to think dating would be fun
    now I'm out here wondering what I've done wrong
    why does my love life feel like a Radiohead song.
    I try to do better for people to see
    but they just wind up ignoring me
    no one to turn to, and no one to help
    at this point I do nothing for myself
    no matter the time no matter the occasion
    I'll still seek a way to strive for validation.

· · · ·

"We can't be together you look kinda funny"
    thanks, now I'll starve myself until my bones get runny
    remember when life was only about toys
    now boys stress the girls, the girls stress the boys
    people can't fall asleep without white noise
    missing the life that internet destroyed

countless days and countless nights
lost by the impact of dating sites
offering help out of feeling alone
only to have your morals overthrown
offering to make you social, pull you out the life of books
just to make you forever wonder about your looks
ignore your face and the fact your room's a mess
the threat of someone coming has you in a constant stress.
You think others think you're lame
cause of your constant stress and sadness
for your ruined sense of image
straight up descending into madness
there's only one thing to blame
it's sites that claim to cause no damage
dating sites and porn
make people wish they wer not born...

WHAT IS UP THERE

Eyes wide open when I'm sleeping
in the corner it is peeping
from the back I feel it creeping
I know it's not that deep
but it is watching me sleep
it is urging me to rise
it is seeing my demise
living scared of every weekend
cause of some critter from the deep end.
The solitude of my room
feels eerily nice
suddenly like "kaboom"
I see my shadow appears twice
why does it follow me
what could it possibly want
does it want to show me
something or does it just taunt
this is not making me better
and no this not flaunting
behind every letter
of this poem lay something haunting.
Does anyone else hear it?
feel like I'm slowly getting near it
every time I leave a crowd
it stars calling for me loud
wish to see it clearer
I could use a magic mirror.
I feel like it plagues me
it's something I can't fight
and I know things like this usually don't end alright

I feel like it plagues me
and it makes me pretty sad
cause something's always watching
and that something wants me dead.
I feel like it plagues me and I've never seen its head
just its shadow and its voice
and the terrifying noise
as it's getting pretty close
leaves me with no choice
but to call for holy ghost...

THE SMILING GLASS

Like a known caller
        the glass on the table calls my name
        if I drink the juice of colour
        the night won't be the same
        in the glass there's stuff to make me happy
        forget for one night that life is crappy
        be it brown or be it blue
        it makes me do what I don't wanna do
        makes me feel like I'm not boring
        but I'll regret all that next morning
        gets me feeling like a star
        feeling like I own the bar
        spending cash, going hard
        next day I can't use my card
        liquor of all kinds and colours
        makes me treat all men like brothers
        to the bar I call all boys in
        get togheter drink more poison
        drink up and calm all inner voices
        drink up and make horrid choices
        drink up ignore all our pain
        may not a drop fall in vain
        Drink up make it feel like rain!
        The morning after doesn't feel nice
        my body feels cold as ice
        I'm seeing everything move twice
        my skin feels as if plagued by mice
        nothing feels right
        my bedsheets feel tight
        apparently I threw up on a flight attendant

I shiver in fright
at this unpleasant sight
of a man like me being alcohol dependent
every weekend the glass is calling my name
every weekend I know it's gonna end the same
chasing strangers in the hopes of fame
drinking looking for a gene to blame
maybe the fault's on my father's ship
for always letting me have a sip
of whatever he had in his cup
it never got me fucked up
but later in early adulthood
discovered i love it more than food
once again the glass smiles
but I'm waking miles and miles
just do avoid kissing it
if I do than I'd be missing it
the glass Is calling louder and louder
to decline it's call I can't be prouder...

It's just a low
    it can't ruin my fun
    so I don't know
    why is my hand on a glass of rum
    i drove through hell and back and still
    I don't have a knack why love can kill
    life is like running up a hill
    although its steep and smells like a landfill.
    Feeling like life is a bitch
    but now the bottle is in my reach
    don't know how did I get in this club
    just how hard did I have to fuck up
    who the hell are those people around me
    how the hell have they even found me
    I see myself dancing with death
    hear it begging for my breath
    is this gasp of air really my last?
    I ask the reaper with his hand on my chest
    friday night just booze and fun
    shots shots shots till I see the sun.
    "Gentlemen,
    let us all take a shot in honour
    for a man

        who used to be a regular now he's a goner".

AUTHOR'S MESSAGE

Dear reader

Once again thank you for reading this work, hope you felt as good reading it as I felt making this.

I've really put a piece of myself into each word so this creation is really a work of pride and dedication.

Big thanks to a lot of people without whom this wouldn't happen (they know who they are) and how else to end this message than with a wish of all good into your life with encouragement to await my future writings I bid farewell to you

[1] „A semi colon[1] is used when an author[2] chooses to end their sentence[3] but doesn't. In this case, the author is

you and the sentence is your life"

62

---

1.   https://www.urbandictionary.com/define.php?term=semi%20colon

2.   https://www.urbandictionary.com/define.php?term=author

3.   https://www.urbandictionary.com/define.php?term=sentence